I0711844

Authors acknowledgment

First and foremost, I would want to thank everyone who has helped and encouraged me in authoring this book, "Same Love, Mismo Amor: A Journey to Self-Acceptance.". Your steadfast conviction in our endeavor has provided inspiration and strength along this journey.

Thank you, family and friends, for their unending love, support, and understanding. Your support and tolerance have been essential, and your belief in me and the work has kept me going.

Finally, I want to thank the readers for taking the time to read this book. I hope it provides you with understanding, compassion, and inspiration. May it help you embrace your genuine self and inspire you to share love and acceptance in your own.

With gratitude,
Eric Zane Moon

TABLE OF CONTENTS

INTRODUCTION

Introduction 1

CHAPTER 1

Understanding Self-Acceptance 17

The importance of self-acceptance and self-love 19

Myths and Misconceptions 21

Practical Steps to Foster Self-Acceptance 23

CHAPTER 2

The Journey Begins 25

Overcoming Internal Barriers 26

Finding the Courage to Live Authentically 28

CHAPTER 3

Cultural and Social Influences 30

Navigating Social Expectations 32

Case Studies and Personal Stories 33

Strategies for Embracing Your True Self within Your Culture 34

CHAPTER 4

Stories of Courage and Resilience 35

Overcoming Societal Prejudice 37

Lessons Learned from Each Journey 38

CHAPTER 5

Tools and Strategies for Self-Acceptance 39

Mindfulness and Meditation 42

Building a Positive Self-Image 43

CHAPTER 6

Overcoming External Challenges 47

Strategies for Dealing with Discrimination and Prejudice 49

Developing a Supportive Environment 51

Personal Stories of Overcoming Discrimination 53

CHAPTER 7

Celebrating Your Identity 54

Personal Strategies for Embracing Diversity and Inclusion 55

The Role of Allies in Promoting Inclusion 57

Celebrating Diversity and Inclusion 58

Positive Impacts of Embracing Diversity and Inclusion 59

CHAPTER 8

Maintaining Self-Acceptance 60

The Role of Self-Reflection 62

Strategies for Continual Growth and Self-Reflection 63

Navigating Setbacks and Challenges 65

Creating a Supportive Environment 66

CONCLUSION

Reflecting on Your Journey 67

Moving Forward with Confidence 68

Final Words of Encouragement 70

Parting Shot 71

INTRODUCTION

If you're reading this, you've likely heard the stories of Adam and Eve versus Adam and Steve, where it's said that God created the former, not the latter. But how true and practical is this narrative? From my experience, these tales may seem interesting and plausible in movies, but they often prove unrealistic in real life.

It's easy to sit on the sidelines, point fingers, and judge. However, the harsh reality for many people involves daily self-hatred and the relentless "Why me?" questions. Unfortunately, not everyone survives this battle, with some tragically resorting to suicide to end what they perceive as their miserable lives. While it may seem that nobody cares, I'm not suggesting they should or shouldn't. The truth of their struggle is known only to them.

As a parent, try to imagine what your child might be enduring in this daily fight against what they perceive as a demon. If you were in their shoes, would you survive it? This is a topic for another day, but the least we can do is offer support. Whether it's a sibling, child, or friend, strive to understand their struggle. It may not be your job, and you might think it has nothing to do with you. If that's the case, you have no business being in that person's life.

Everyone in this world needs love, regardless of its source. Even you, my precious reader, need love. That's why we have families, friends, soul mates, partners, spouses, husbands, and wives. Love is a matter of the heart. So why judge someone's pursuit of love and play God by dictating their source of love based on gender, colour, race, or tribe? Get off your high horse, respect other people's lives, and let them live as they choose. Tomorrow is unknown, so let them control what they can control today.

My precious reader, I love you to the moon and back. Remember that. Now go ahead and share that love while you still can. You don't want to live with regrets.

HAPPY READING!!

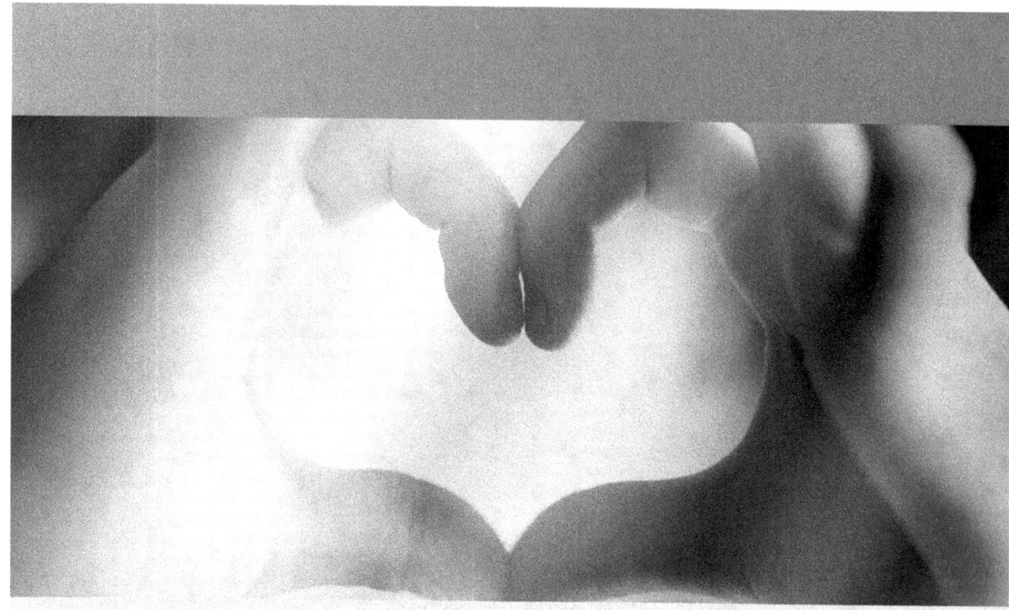

Preface

Welcome to "Same Love, Mismo Amor: A Journey of Self-Acceptance." This book was written out of a genuine desire to promote love, acceptance, and understanding in a society where love is frequently misunderstood and marginalized.

In our society, love stories have long been influenced by stereotypes and preconceived assumptions. The well-known narrative of Adam and Eve vs. Adam and Steve illustrates how deeply ingrained these biases can be. However, while these tales are popular in media and culture, they frequently fail to capture the complex, wonderful reality of human relationships and the various ways in which people feel love.

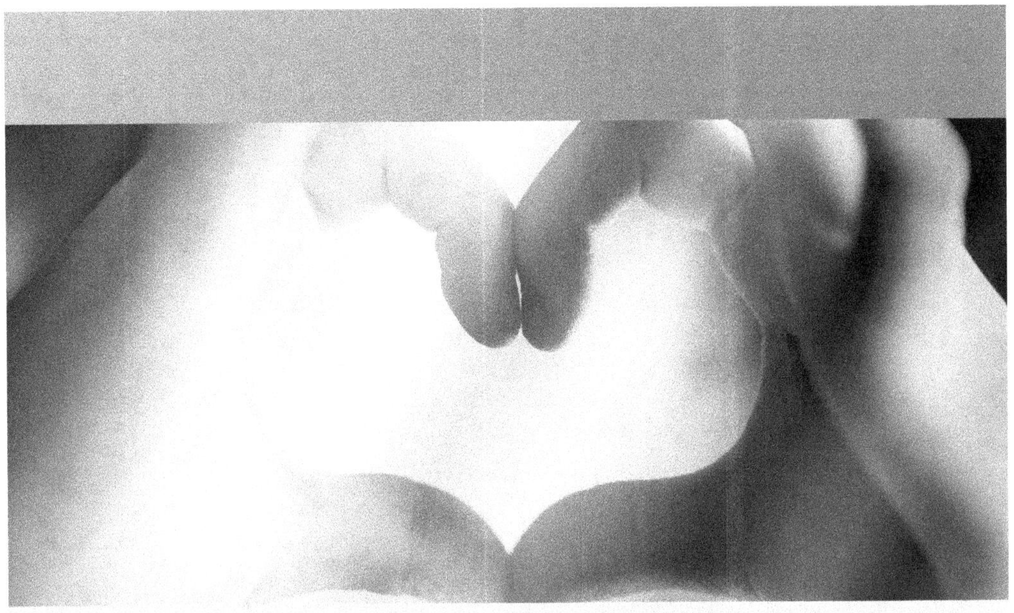

Throughout this book, we will delve into the importance of understanding and accepting one's sexuality. We will explore the journey to self-acceptance, the challenges faced by those who love differently, and the undeniable truth that love in all its forms is essential to the human experience. By sharing personal stories, scientific insights, and practical advice, my goal is to help you, the reader, navigate your path to understanding and acceptance.

This book is not just for those who are coming to terms with their sexuality but also for parents, friends, siblings, and allies who seek to support their loved ones. It is a call to empathy and compassion, urging everyone to look beyond societal expectations and see the person behind the labels.

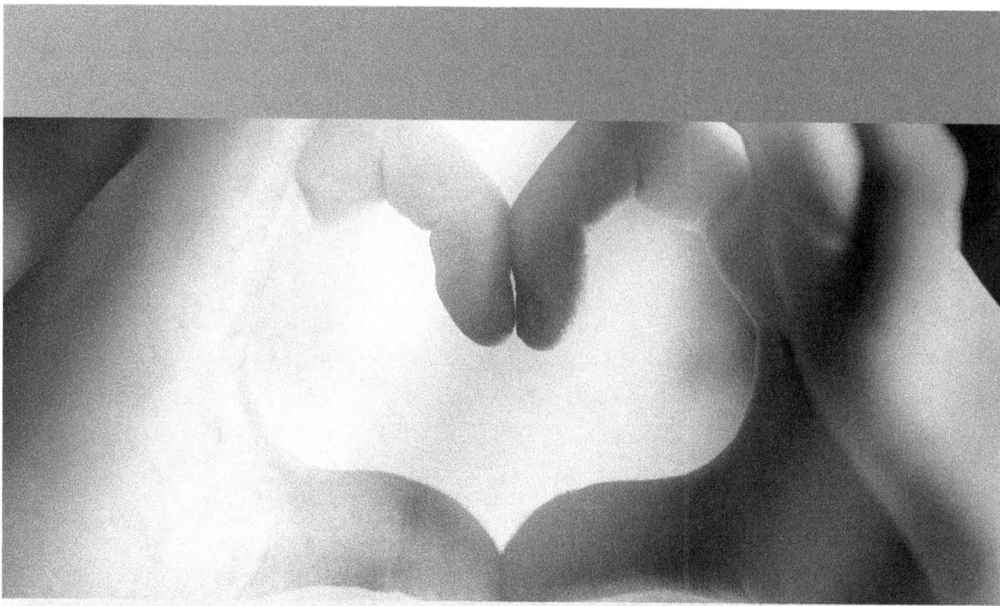

We all need love. It is a fundamental part of what makes us human. Whether it comes from family, friends, partners, or within ourselves, love is the driving force behind our happiness and well-being. Yet, despite its universal importance, many people still face discrimination and rejection because of whom they love. This book aims to challenge that injustice and advocate for a world where love is celebrated in all its forms.

As you read through these pages, I hope you will open your heart and mind to new perspectives. Let us move beyond judgement and embrace a more inclusive understanding of love. For love is love, no matter its form, and every person deserves to experience it fully and freely.

Thank you for embarking on this journey with me. Together, we can create a more loving and accepting world.

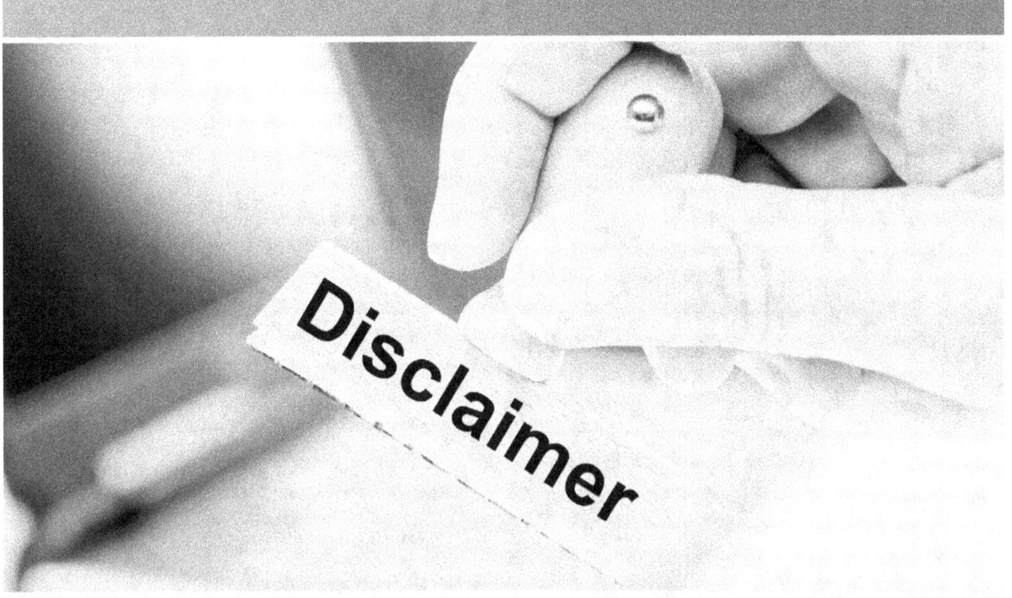

The content of this ebook, "Same Love, Mismo Amor: A Journey of Self-Acceptance," is intended for informational and educational purposes only. The views, opinions, and advice expressed herein are those of the author and do not necessarily reflect the official policy or position of any other individual or organization.

This ebook aims to foster understanding and acceptance of diverse sexual orientations and relationships. However, it is not a substitute for professional advice, diagnosis, or treatment. Readers are encouraged to seek the counsel of qualified professionals for any personal, medical, or psychological issues they may face.

The personal stories and experiences shared in this ebook are intended to provide insights and foster empathy. They are not meant to represent every individual's experience. Each person's journey with their sexuality and identity is unique.

The author has made every effort to ensure the accuracy and completeness of the information provided. However, the author assumes no responsibility or liability for any errors, omissions, or inaccuracies in the content. Any action you take based on the information in this ebook is strictly at your own risk.

This ebook also discusses social and legal issues related to sexuality and relationships. Laws and social attitudes vary widely by location and may change over time. Readers are advised to stay informed about the legal and social context in their own areas.

The purpose of this ebook is to promote love, acceptance, and understanding. The author respects all perspectives and encourages respectful dialogue and consideration of diverse viewpoints.

Fun facts about the History

Ancient Recognition

Same-sex partnerships were quite prevalent and frequently honoured in ancient Greece. The Greeks held that "platonic love" encompassed strong intellectual and emotional ties shared by individuals of the same sex.

Roman Connections

Same-sex partnerships had a history in the Roman Empire as well. Roman Emperor Hadrian was famously in love with a young Greek man named Antinous and had even named a city after him.

People with Two Spirits

Two Spirit persons, who embodied both masculine and feminine aspects, were acknowledged and respected by numerous Native American societies. In their societies, they frequently occupied revered positions as spiritual guides and healers.

Medieval Europe

Although same-sex relationships were generally frowned upon in mediaeval Europe, there were nonetheless cases of openly acknowledged same-sex love. For example, the relationship between King Edward II of England and Piers Gaveston was widely acknowledged.

Renaissance Love

During the Renaissance, several prominent figures, including artists and writers, were known to have same-sex relationships. Michelangelo and Leonardo da Vinci are believed to have had romantic relationships with men, as reflected in their letters and artworks.

Boston Marriages

In the 19th and early 20th centuries, some women in the United States entered into "Boston marriages," living together in long-term, committed relationships without marrying men. These relationships were often deeply affectionate and romantic.

Walt Whitman's Poetry

The famous American poet Walt Whitman celebrated same-sex love in his poetry. His collection "Leaves of Grass" contains numerous references to the beauty and depth of love between men.

The Pink Triangle

During World War II, the Nazis forced gay men to wear pink triangles as a form of identification and persecution. This symbol was later reclaimed by the LGBTQ+ community as a symbol of pride and resistance.

Harvey Milk's Legacy

Harvey Milk, one of the first openly gay elected officials in the United States, played a crucial role in the fight for LGBTQ+ rights in the 1970s. His activism and tragic assassination in 1978 helped galvanize the movement for equality.

Marriage Equality Milestones

The Netherlands became the first country to legalize same-sex marriage in 2001. Since then, many other countries have followed suit, reflecting growing acceptance and recognition of the same love around the world.

The Stonewall Riots

The Stonewall Riots of 1969 in New York City marked a pivotal moment in the LGBTQ+ rights movement. This event, led by members of the LGBTQ+ community, sparked widespread activism and is commemorated annually with Pride Month celebrations.

Iconic Literature

Many classic literary works feature themes of same-sex love, often subtly due to the social constraints of their times. For example, Virginia Woolf's "Orlando" and James Baldwin's "Giovanni's Room" are celebrated for their exploration of same-sex relationships.

Influential Activists

Throughout history, many activists have fought for the rights and recognition of the same love. Figures like Marsha P. Johnson and Sylvia Rivera, prominent in the early LGBTQ+ rights movement, played crucial roles in advocating for transgender and gay rights.

Cultural Representation

Various cultures have their own unique histories and traditions regarding the same love. In Japan, for example, the Edo period saw the flourishing of "wakashudo," or the "way of the young," which involved same-sex relationships between samurai and their apprentices.

Modern Milestones

Recent decades have seen significant progress in the fight for the same love recognition and rights. The legalization of same-sex marriage in numerous countries, increasing representation in media, and the growing visibility of LGBTQ+ people in all walks of life are testaments to this progress.

Fun facts about the Present

Global Marriage Equality

As of 2024, over 30 countries have legalized same-sex marriage, reflecting growing global acceptance. Countries like the Netherlands, Canada, South Africa, and Taiwan are pioneers in recognizing marriage equality.

Pride Parades Worldwide

Pride parades, which began as a form of protest, are now celebrated globally with millions of participants. Cities like São Paulo, New York, and Madrid host some of the largest Pride events, showcasing the vibrancy and diversity of the LGBTQ+ community.

Increased Representation in Media

LGBTQ+ characters and storylines are becoming more common in mainstream media. Popular TV shows like "Schitt's Creek," "Pose," and "Orange Is the New Black" have received critical acclaim for their authentic and diverse representations.

Celebrity Advocates

Many celebrities openly support and advocate for LGBTQ+ rights. Figures like Ellen DeGeneres, Laverne Cox, Lil Nas X, and Troye Sivan use their platforms to promote acceptance and equality.

Corporate Support

Many major corporations now actively support LGBTQ+ rights and inclusivity. Companies like Google, Apple, and Nike regularly participate in Pride events and have policies promoting diversity and inclusion in the workplace.

Legal Protections

Many countries and regions have implemented laws protecting LGBTQ+ individuals from discrimination in areas such as employment, housing, and public services. The European Union, for instance, has comprehensive anti-discrimination legislation.

LGBTQ+ Youth Advocacy

Organizations like The Trevor Project and It Gets Better Project focus on supporting LGBTQ+ youth, providing resources, crisis intervention, and fostering a sense of community and hope.

Health and Wellness

There is growing awareness and research focused on the specific health needs of the LGBTQ+ community. Initiatives addressing mental health, HIV/AIDS prevention, and overall wellness are becoming more prevalent.

Sports Inclusion

The world of sports is becoming more inclusive, with openly LGBTQ+ athletes like Megan Rapinoe, Adam Rippon, and Gus Kenworthy challenging stereotypes and advocating for equality.

Academic Recognition

Universities and schools are increasingly including LGBTQ+ studies in their curricula, fostering a deeper understanding of the community's history, struggles, and contributions.

Transgender Rights Movement

The transgender rights movement is gaining momentum, with significant strides in legal recognition and social acceptance. Countries like Argentina and Pakistan have implemented progressive laws supporting transgender individuals.

Global Advocacy

International organizations like the United Nations and Amnesty International actively campaign for LGBTQ+ rights worldwide, addressing issues such as violence, discrimination, and legal inequalities.

Online Communities

Social media and online platforms provide vital spaces for LGBTQ+ individuals to connect, share their experiences, and advocate for their rights. Platforms like Instagram, TikTok, and Twitter have vibrant LGBTQ+ communities.

Intersectional Advocacy

There is a growing emphasis on intersectionality within the LGBTQ+ movement, recognizing the overlapping struggles related to race, gender, class, and sexuality. Activists are increasingly advocating for a more inclusive and holistic approach to equality.

Youth Empowerment

Younger generations are more open and accepting of diverse sexual orientations and gender identities. Studies show that Gen Z is the most LGBTQ+ inclusive generation yet, with many young people actively advocating for equal rights.

Fun facts about the Future

Expanding Marriage Equality

As societal acceptance continues to grow, it's anticipated that more countries will legalize same-sex marriage. This could lead to a future where marriage equality is the global standard.

Universal Anti-Discrimination Laws

Future legislation is likely to increasingly protect LGBTQ+ individuals from discrimination in all areas of life, including employment, healthcare, and education, creating a more inclusive and equitable society worldwide.

Advances in Representation

 Media and entertainment will likely continue to expand their representation of LGBTQ+ characters and stories, providing more diverse and authentic portrayals that resonate with a wider audience.

Technological Connectivity

Advances in technology and social media will provide even more platforms for LGBTQ+ individuals to connect, support each other, and advocate for their rights, fostering a global community of allies and activists.

Inclusive Education

Schools and universities will increasingly incorporate comprehensive LGBTQ+ history and studies into their curricula, promoting understanding and acceptance from a young age and preparing future generations to be more inclusive.

Corporate Leadership

More businesses are expected to champion LGBTQ+ rights, implement policies that promote diversity and inclusion, and support LGBTQ+ initiatives, making workplace equality a norm rather than an exception.

Healthcare Innovations

Future advancements in healthcare will likely address the specific needs of the LGBTQ+ community more effectively, with tailored mental health services, improved access to hormone therapy, and enhanced HIV/AIDS treatment and prevention.

Global Advocacy Networks

International cooperation and advocacy will likely strengthen, with organizations working together across borders to promote LGBTQ+ rights, share resources, and support communities in regions where acceptance is still growing.

Intersectional Movements

The future of LGBTQ+ advocacy will increasingly embrace intersectionality, addressing the interconnected issues of race, gender, socioeconomic status, and sexual orientation to ensure a more comprehensive approach to equality.

Youth Leadership

Young activists and leaders from the LGBTQ+ community will continue to rise, using their voices and platforms to drive change, influence policy, and inspire future generations to embrace diversity and inclusion.

Legal Recognition of Non-Binary Identities

More countries will likely recognize non-binary and gender non-conforming identities legally, providing appropriate documentation options and protections under the law.

Parental Rights and Family Structures

Legal recognition of diverse family structures will expand, ensuring that LGBTQ+ parents have equal rights and protections and that children in these families are supported and valued.

Community Centers and Safe Spaces

The establishment of more LGBTQ+ community centres and safe spaces will provide essential resources, support, and social opportunities, fostering stronger and more resilient communities.

Cultural Shift

As acceptance continues to grow, cultural narratives around love and relationships will evolve, normalizing the same love in all aspects of life and reducing stigma and prejudice.

CHAPTER 1

Understanding Self-Acceptance

Now I know that you might be asking yourself this question that lingers in one's mind about self-acceptance, and how do you go about that? Well, let me tell you, my beloved reader, the moment you acknowledge the fact that sexuality is an integral part of our lives, unfortunately, you have to be within one of its categories.

The good thing you can do for yourself is accept your sexuality, and only then will you start understanding and accepting yourself. Nobody, and I repeat nobody, was born perfect; we all have our imperfections; it's just that others seem to notice some people's flaws more than those of theirs. Nobody gets to choose how they want to be born in terms of sexuality; if we had, we were all going to choose the normal hetero way of life.

Understanding these elements of life contributes to one's unique identity and resilience towards anything that life throws their way.

Self-acceptance does boost your self-confidence and esteem in whatever sphere of life you might find yourself in. Opinions should always remain as simple as that, and let's respect other people's because they are not yours and they do not make you who you are.

The importance of self-acceptance and self-love

Accepting and loving oneself is often linked to reduced anxiety and depression. Which brings about confidence in oneself, a more positive outlook on life, and better mental well-being.

So practising more of these elements helps one stay mentally sharp and unfazed by the challenges of life. Individuals who practise self-acceptance are better equipped to handle life's challenges and setbacks. They are less likely to be swayed by external opinions and more likely to remain grounded during tough times and tend to respect other people.

In relationships, there seems to be longevity in those who have accepted and love themselves because it's easy to love the next person if you love yourself enough. Working on yourself is very imperative, for you will see in yourself what you would want other people to see in you, and they are bound to accept and love you for that.

Personal growth is a journey that one embarks on over time.Life goals will be achievable without the fear of failure because you now know that failure is a part of life, not an obstacle.

Myths and Misconceptions

Some believe that accepting oneself means giving up on self-improvement. However, true self-acceptance is about recognizing and embracing oneself while still striving for personal growth and betterment.This is because they either do not understand the self-acceptance on their own or they are just ignorant which most could just be that, ignorant.

Accepting oneself is not about being self-centred. It is about developing a healthy relationship with oneself, which in turn can enhance one's ability to contribute positively to others.after all one needs to be selfish once in a while if not always , jokes , laugh a little it does go a long way.

Achieving self-acceptance is a continuous process that requires effort, reflection, and patience. It is not a one-time achievement but an ongoing journey. It will all make sense once you have self-acceptance and self-love because you will be brimming with confidence and exuding love.

Practical Steps to Foster Self-Acceptance

Regularly take time to reflect on your thoughts, feelings, and actions. Journaling can be a helpful tool in this process because you can write just about anything, even the things that you will not be able to discuss with others. I know this may sound foreign and or taboo but it will come naturally once you get that pen and paper to jot down on.

Engage in mindfulness or meditation to cultivate awareness and non-judgmental observation of your thoughts and emotions.Use affirmations to counter negative self-talk and reinforce positive beliefs about yourself.Connect with supportive friends, family, or professionals who encourage your journey towards self-acceptance.

Prioritise activities and practices that nurture your well-being, such as exercise, hobbies, and rest and I can not emphasise enough on exercising and resting enough after it all, it does wonders for your mindset.

CHAPTER 2

The Journey Begins

We have talked about self-acceptance and self-love, now let's talk about embracing your sexuality and your true self. Now this is where you get to let life take its course and let life be without having to fight it. Life will lead the right people to your direction effortlessly without you even trying or lifting a finger.

This is where you get to distinguish between people who are your ride or die and you would want to stick with them to continue feeding yourself with true love. We need to learn to nurture everything that blooms and right here you would have built a circle to keep and nurture.Let everything toxic go let them be part of your life from a distance, and let them watch you from the fence, you do not have to force them to be part of your life.

Overcoming Internal Barriers

You will have your inner voice and gut feeling and learn to listen to the former and follow the latter. Guardian angels that you have been blocking all this while will have now found a way to communicate with you , all you need to do is let them take charge and you follow the lead.

Yes, there will be times when you will need some kind of assurance from people from time to time but do not be alarmed by that. That is part of the battles of life that we face every day and smile about it and make life worth living.do not forget to forgive those who might have called you names , they are only human and mistakes make people human , only the immortal have the luxury of giving their tongue to the cat.

So people will not stop judging but you can stop giving them the satisfaction and your precious time, if they can talk ill about it they claim to love what about you.Seek support and help wherever it is you fall short, that's why you have your support system use it to your advantage.Now go out there and have fun do not limit yourself to possibilities of life by letting the internal barriers overcome you, the inverse is true.

Finding the Courage to Live Authentically

Recognize and celebrate what makes you unique. Embrace your individuality and understand that your differences are your strengths.Use positive affirmations to reinforce your self-worth and confidence. Remind yourself daily of your value and capabilities. That you matter to people who matter to you and do everything in your power to keep them.

Ensure that your actions align with your core values and beliefs. Living authentically means making choices that reflect your true self.Understand that vulnerability is a strength, not a weakness. Allow yourself to be open and honest, even if it feels uncomfortable.Honesty is the best policy and people appreciate honesty and they will reciprocate that tenfold.

Seek out relationships with people who accept and support your true self. Positive relationships provide encouragement and strength.Look for role models and mentors who exemplify authenticity. Their experiences and guidance can inspire and support your journey.They do not have to be celebrities or public figures but just people that have been doing this long enough to guide you wherever you need help.

CHAPTER 3

Cultural and Social Influences

Culture plays a significant role into our upbringing , values, self-perception, and identity.It's through culture that one gets to learn about identities and how to present themselves before society and all.With certain things one is not supposed to do and adhere to and what not to do because it reflects bad on them. You are at a stage where you now can filter what works for you and what does not and make informed decisions.

There are cultural rules that one has to follow and abide by and truly speaking some have groomed and shaped us into the people we are today. Although there are those that are questionable, the best way is to do what works best for you because at the end of the day, it's your life you are living and gambling with and you will not be able to replace it.

Family is often the first source of cultural norms and values. From a young age, we learn about behaviours and beliefs through our family's teachings and actions and we take that with us wherever we go and grow with them engraved in us.

Schools, media, and other societal institutions reinforce cultural norms and values. These sources shape our understanding of what is considered "normal" or "ideal." This is everything we know to this date and that is what is still holding people back, they do not want to change, not to mention the system they only grew up knowing to be the only truth about life.

Navigating Social Expectations

Engage in self-reflection to identify the cultural norms and values that have influenced your self-perception. Consider how these influences align with your true self.Embrace and celebrate aspects of your culture that resonate with your authentic self. Cultural pride can enhance self-esteem and a sense of identity.Embrace and celebrate aspects of your culture that resonate with your authentic self. Cultural pride can enhance self-esteem and a sense of identity.

Seek support from individuals and communities who understand and respect your journey to self-acceptance. Allies can provide encouragement and validation.Consider seeking guidance from therapists or counsellors who specialise in cultural issues. They can offer strategies for navigating cultural expectations while maintaining self-acceptance.

Case Studies and Personal Stories

An individual from a collectivist culture navigates the tension between family expectations and personal desires.A person from a culture with rigid gender roles embraces a non-binary identity and finds self-acceptance.

These stories highlight the resilience and adaptability of individuals as they navigate cultural influences on their self-perception. Embracing one's true self, even in the face of cultural expectations, leads to empowerment and a stronger sense of identity.

Strategies for Embracing Your True Self within Your Culture

Educate yourself about your culture's history, values, and norms. Awareness can help you understand the roots of cultural expectations.Develop an understanding of other cultures and perspectives. This can broaden your view and provide alternative ways of thinking and being.

Practice assertiveness in expressing your needs and boundaries. Communicate your authentic self clearly and confidently.Advocate for cultural change and inclusivity within your community. Support initiatives that promote diversity and acceptance.

Create a personal narrative that integrates your cultural identity with your authentic self. This narrative should reflect your unique journey and values.Share your story with others to foster understanding and connection. Storytelling can be a powerful tool for personal and cultural transformation.

CHAPTER 4

Stories of Courage and Resilience

Personal stories from diverse backgrounds of an individual growing up in a conservative, collectivist culture where family honour and societal expectations are paramount.The protagonist struggles with the pressure to conform to traditional gender roles and career paths while grappling with their own identity and aspirations.

The protagonist experiences internal conflict between their authentic self and the cultural expectations imposed upon them. This leads to feelings of guilt, confusion, and fear of disappointing loved ones.A pivotal moment occurs when the protagonist decides to pursue their passion for art, despite familial opposition. They find solace and support in a community of like-minded individuals who encourage their self-expression.

The protagonist learns to accept and embrace their true self, finding a balance between honouring their cultural heritage and living authentically. By sharing their story, they inspire others within their cultural community to question traditional norms and pursue their own paths to self-acceptance.

Overcoming Societal Prejudice

An individual from a marginalised community facing systemic discrimination and societal prejudice based on their race, sexual orientation, or disability.The protagonist confronts daily microaggressions, bias, and exclusion, leading to struggles with self-worth and identity.

Despite the challenges, the protagonist demonstrates resilience by seeking out supportive networks and advocacy groups that affirm their identity and fight for equality.

Lessons Learned from Each Journey

Each story highlights the resilience and courage required to navigate the journey to self-acceptance. Despite diverse backgrounds and challenges, these individuals demonstrate the power of perseverance. The importance of finding supportive communities and allies is a recurring theme.Support networks play a crucial role in fostering self-acceptance and providing validation.

Embracing authenticity leads to empowerment and a stronger sense of self. These stories
show that living authentically, despite societal pressures, is key to achieving self-acceptance.
Balancing cultural heritage with personal authenticity can lead to a richer and more fulfilling identity.Recognizing and embracing intersectional identities is crucial for understanding and celebrating the complexity of self.Healing from trauma is an essential part of the journey to self-acceptance, and self-compassion is vital in this process.

CHAPTER 5

Tools and Strategies for Self-Acceptance

Practical Exercises and Techniques include Self-Reflection and Journaling that's where you will get to learn what is it you can improve towards as human and work at your flaws.It does not have to take too much of your time, it can even be less than 5 minutes but it is all worth it as it will help grow individually.

It does not have to be about deep stuff, it can be just about anything from where it is you find solace and who it is you look up to. Work on past mistakes and work on becoming a better person towards everyone, what drives you up the wall, what you will want to change about it, and where you think you need help.

Set aside 10-15 minutes each day to write about your thoughts, feelings, and experiences. Focus on self-reflection and self-discovery.Use prompts such as "What did I learn about myself today?" or "How did I handle a challenging situation?" to guide your writing.Write down three things you are grateful for each day.

This practice helps shift your focus to positive aspects of your life and promotes self-appreciation.It can be more than three things but remember that what is above it all is life itself and then wisdom to be able to distinguish between right and wrong, the reason to forgive and forget then with these principles of life you should be able to accomplish a complete life.Reflect on why you are grateful for these things and how they contribute to your well-being.

When you experience self-criticism or negative thoughts, write them down. Then, respond to these thoughts with compassion and kindness as if you were comforting a friend. Use phrases like "It's okay to make mistakes" or "I am worthy of love and acceptance" to counteract negative self-talk.

Work on positive self-talk that will eventually give you solace and comfort.Do not try to be an Iron because that leads to you being toxic towards others especially those who love you wholeheartedly so, try and tackle issues as they come, and try not to bottle things up, you will thank me later.

Mindfulness and Meditation

Practise mindful breathing to stay present and reduce stress. Focus on your breath, observing each inhale and exhale without judgement.Try a simple breathing pattern, such as inhaling for four counts, holding for four counts, and exhaling for four counts. Repeat this cycle for 5-10 minutes.

Perform a body scan meditation to connect with your body and release tension. Lie down or sit comfortably and bring your attention to different parts of your body, starting from your toes and moving up to your head.As you focus on each body part, notice any sensations without trying to change them. Simply observe and accept what you feel.

Practise loving-kindness meditation to cultivate self-love and compassion. Sit quietly and repeat phrases like "May I be happy, may I be healthy, may I be safe, may I live with ease. Gradually extend these wishes to others, including loved ones, acquaintances, and even those with whom you have conflicts.

Building a Positive Self-Image

Create a list of positive affirmations that resonate with you and repeat them daily. These statements should be empowering and reflect your desired self-perception. Place affirmations where you can see them, such as on your mirror or as reminders on your phone.

Examples include "I am worthy of love and respect" and "I embrace my unique qualities. This can be a lot to put up with but there's no hurt in trying some of these things, you will only have yourself to thank.Visualize your ideal self and the life you want to create.

Spend a few minutes each day imagining yourself living confidently and authentically. Use all your senses to make the visualization vivid. Picture yourself achieving your goals, feeling happy, and embracing your true self. If you can imagine it then you can do it and bring it to life, you just need to train your brain and mind to think positively.

Develop a self-care routine that includes activities you enjoy and that nurture your well-being. This routine should address physical, emotional, and mental health. Schedule regular self-care activities such as exercise, hobbies, relaxation, and socializing. Prioritize these activities as essential parts of your life.

Identify negative thoughts and challenge their validity. Replace them with more balanced and positive perspectives. Our mind feeds from whatever it is we feed it, if you concentrate on feeding good thoughts and positive stuff, it is bound to feed you positive things back to you.
Use a thought record worksheet to document negative thoughts, evidence for and against them, and alternative, more positive thoughts.

Test out new behaviours and observe their outcomes to challenge negative beliefs. For example, if you believe you are not likeable, engage in social activities and note positive
interactions. Plan and execute small experiments, then reflect on the results to reinforce positive self-beliefs.Participate in support groups where you can share experiences and receive encouragement from others facing similar challenges.

This does not have to be formal, you can look for groups on social media if you do not have any around your neck of the woods. Look for local or online groups focused on self-acceptance, mental health, or specific issues you are dealing with.Work with a therapist or counsellor to explore deeper issues and develop personalized strategies for self-acceptance.

For an alternative look for anyone in your neighbourhood who can be of any help you do not necessarily have to be candid about everything you can just ask for help by posing as a concerned friend. Engage in regular sessions and be open to discussing your thoughts and feelings. Therapy can provide a safe space for growth and healing.

CHAPTER 6

Understanding Self-Acceptance

Dealing with Discrimination and Prejudice is what you will encounter at some point in your life whether you want it or are ready for it, you might as well brace yourself for it dark or no dinner. However that won't affect your life as long as you don't let it, sticking to your guns will always go a long way. Keep calm and remind yourself of the most important things in life.

Unfair treatment based on characteristics such as race, gender, sexual orientation, disability, or religion.Preconceived opinions or attitudes about an individual or group that are not based on reason or experience.

Cultural norms and stereotypes perpetuate discriminatory attitudes and behaviors. Fear of the unknown and lack of understanding often lead to prejudice. Historical events and power dynamics contribute to systemic discrimination.

Constant exposure to discrimination can lead to chronic stress and anxiety. Internalizing negative messages from society can erode self-esteem and self-worth. Prolonged discrimination can contribute to feelings of hopelessness and depression. Now this is a serious issue that has stolen a lot of our brothers and sisters in silence, please be loud about it and do not let it overcome you no matter what the circumstances.

Discrimination can lead to social exclusion and isolation from supportive communities. Discriminatory practices in the workplace and education can limit opportunities for financial stability and growth.

Strategies for Dealing with Discrimination and Prejudice

Prioritise self-care practices to maintain your mental and emotional well-being. Engage in activities that rejuvenate and strengthen you. Counteract negative societal messages with positive affirmations and self-talk. Remind yourself of your worth and capabilities. Practice mindfulness, meditation, and other stress management techniques to stay grounded and reduce anxiety.

Surround yourself with friends, family, and communities that affirm and support your identity. Professional counseling can provide a safe space to process experiences of discrimination and develop coping strategies. Join support groups where you can share experiences and receive encouragement from others who have faced similar challenges.

Educate yourself about the history and dynamics of discrimination and prejudice. Understanding the context can empower you to challenge these attitudes. My precious reader this is not compulsory do it if it feels good and educative, if it's not do not force it.

Get involved in advocacy and activism to fight against discrimination and promote inclusivity. Use your voice to raise awareness and push for change. Whilst change is as good as a holiday it can be overwhelming as well so be careful of what you try to implement because there is no turning back my good friend.

Familiarise yourself with your legal rights and protections against discrimination. Organizations such as the ACLU and EEOC provide valuable information and support. Report instances of discrimination to appropriate authorities or organizations. Many places have mechanisms for addressing and rectifying discriminatory practices. Find allies in your workplace, school, or community who can support and advocate for you.

Developing a Supportive Environment

Find allies in your workplace, school, or community who can support and advocate for you. If you are a loner like me don't worry I've got you covered, read and do a lot of reading and writing. Do rely on the old-fashioned way method, it has proved prominent.

Cultivate a home environment that supports and affirms your identity. Surround yourself with symbols and items that make you feel safe and valued. Identify and frequent spaces in the community where you feel accepted and valued. This might include specific social groups, clubs, or organizations.

Use inclusive language and behaviors to promote a culture of acceptance and respect in your interactions. When safe and appropriate, challenge discriminatory comments and behaviors. Educate others about the impact of their words and actions.

Seek out mentors who can offer guidance and support in navigating discrimination and prejudice. Get involved in community organizations and initiatives that promote diversity and inclusion. Building networks of support can provide strength and solidarity.

Personal Stories of Overcoming Discrimination

A young woman from a marginalized racial group faces workplace discrimination. She documents her experiences, seeks legal advice, and joins a support group for women of color in her industry. Through resilience and support, she successfully challenges discriminatory practices at her workplace and advocates for systemic change.

An LGBTQ+ individual experiences social prejudice in their conservative community.
They find solace in online communities, participate in LGBTQ+ advocacy, and educate their peers about LGBTQ+ issues. They build a supportive network and foster a more inclusive environment in their community through persistent education and advocacy.

CHAPTER 7

Celebrating Your Identity

Embracing Diversity and Inclusion is essential for fostering a society where everyone can feel valued and accepted for who they are. The presence of differences within a given setting, encompasses race, ethnicity, gender, age, sexual orientation, disability, and other attributes.Creating an environment where all individuals feel respected, accepted, and valued. Inclusion involves active efforts to ensure that everyone has equal opportunities and access to resources.

Diverse perspectives lead to more creative solutions and innovative ideas. Inclusive environments encourage diverse viewpoints, leading to better decision-making and problem-solving. Embracing diversity and inclusion fosters a sense of belonging and strengthens social cohesion.

Personal Strategies for Embracing Diversity and Inclusion

Take the time to learn about different cultures, traditions, and perspectives. Read books, watch documentaries, and attend cultural events. Acknowledge and reflect on your own biases and stereotypes. Consider how these biases may affect your interactions and attitudes toward others.

Engage in active listening during conversations, especially with people from different backgrounds. Show genuine interest in their experiences and perspectives. Step out of your comfort zone and try new activities or experiences that expose you to different cultures and viewpoints.

Intentionally build relationships with people from diverse backgrounds. Seek out friendships, mentorships, and professional connections that expand your social circle. Advocate for inclusive practices in social settings, such as ensuring everyone has a chance to speak and participate in group activities.

Encourage inclusive practices in your workplace, school, or community organizations. This can include advocating for diversity training, inclusive policies, and equitable opportunities. Get involved in or support initiatives that promote diversity and inclusion. This can involve volunteering, donating, or participating in awareness campaigns.

The Role of Allies in Promoting Inclusion

An ally is someone who actively supports and advocates for marginalized groups, using their privilege to promote equality and inclusion. Allies play a crucial role in creating inclusive environments by amplifying marginalized voices and challenging discriminatory practices.

Continuously educate yourself about the issues and challenges faced by marginalized groups. Stay informed about current events and social justice movements. Use your voice to challenge discriminatory behaviors and advocate for inclusive practices. This includes calling out microaggressions and standing up against injustice. Amplify the voices of marginalized individuals by listening, validating their experiences, and providing platforms for them to share their stories.

Celebrating Diversity and Inclusion

Attend cultural festivals, parades, and celebrations in your community. These events provide opportunities to learn and appreciate different cultures. Acknowledge and celebrate cultural holidays and traditions with your friends and colleagues. This fosters a sense of inclusion and respect for diversity.

Share your own experiences and listen to others' stories about diversity and inclusion. Personal narratives can foster understanding and empathy. Support initiatives that provide platforms for diverse voices to be heard, such as storytelling events, blogs, or social media campaigns.

Use inclusive language that respects and acknowledges diversity. Avoid stereotypes and assumptions based on someone's background or identity. Ensure that everyone has equal access to opportunities and resources. This includes advocating for fair hiring practices, equal pay, and accessible environments.

Positive Impacts of Embracing Diversity and Inclusion

Embracing diversity and inclusion broadens your perspectives and enhances your understanding of the world. Interacting with diverse groups improves your communication and social skills, making you more adaptable and empathetic. Inclusive practices foster deeper and more meaningful connections with others, based on mutual respect and understanding.

Embracing diversity strengthens community bonds and promotes social harmony, reducing prejudice and conflict. Diverse and inclusive workplaces are more innovative and successful, as they harness a wide range of talents and perspectives. In academic settings, diversity enhances collaborative learning and prepares students for a globalized world.

CHAPTER 8

Maintaining Self-Acceptance

Continual Growth and Self-Reflection will all come over time so continue to nurture it and embrace it, it will feel new and unusual but you get used to it eventually. You will be a better person for it and you will notice the changes and it will be for the better try not to rush the process, it's supposed to be gradual.

Lifelong learning is the ongoing pursuit of knowledge and skills throughout an individual's life. It encompasses both formal and informal learning experiences. Continual growth promotes mental agility, adaptability, and resilience. It enriches your life by opening new opportunities and perspectives.

Establish personal development goals that align with your values and aspirations. These goals can range from acquiring new skills to improving emotional intelligence. Seek out opportunities for learning, such as courses, workshops, books, and online resources. Stay curious and open to new experiences.

Cultivate an adaptable mindset that allows you to embrace change and uncertainty. Flexibility in the face of change enhances your ability to grow and evolve. Develop resilience by learning from setbacks and viewing challenges as opportunities for growth. Resilience strengthens your capacity to navigate life's ups and downs.

The Role of Self-Reflection

Set aside time regularly to reflect on your thoughts, feelings, and experiences. This practice helps you gain insights into your behavior and motivations. Use journaling as a tool for self-reflection. Write about your experiences, challenges, and accomplishments to track your personal growth. Periodically review your personal development goals to assess your progress. Adjust your goals as needed to reflect your evolving priorities and aspirations.

Acknowledge and celebrate your achievements, both big and small. Recognizing your progress reinforces positive behavior and motivates further growth. Approach self-criticism constructively by focusing on areas for improvement rather than dwelling on shortcomings. Use this feedback to guide your development. Solicit feedback from trusted friends, mentors, or professionals. External perspectives can provide valuable insights and highlight blind spots.

Strategies for Continual Growth and Self-Reflection

Embrace the belief that your abilities and intelligence can be developed through dedication and hard work. A growth mindset fosters a love for learning and resilience. View challenges as opportunities to learn and grow. Approach difficulties with curiosity and a willingness to overcome obstacles. Practice mindfulness to cultivate present-moment awareness. Being mindful helps you stay attuned to your thoughts and emotions, facilitating self-reflection.

Incorporate meditation into your routine to enhance self-awareness and emotional regulation. Meditation promotes inner peace and clarity.Engage in creative activities such as art, music, writing, or dance. Creative expression can be a powerful tool for self-discovery and emotional release.

Use creativity to approach problems from new angles. Innovative thinking can lead to unique solutions and personal breakthroughs. Surround yourself with supportive and like-minded individuals who encourage your growth and self-acceptance. Seek out mentors who can provide guidance, inspiration, and support. Mentorship can accelerate your personal and professional development.

Navigating Setbacks and Challenges

Recognize that setbacks are a natural part of the growth process. Everyone experiences challenges, and they can provide valuable learning opportunities. Reflect on setbacks to understand what went wrong and how you can improve. Use these experiences to inform your future actions. Focus on intrinsic motivators, such as personal satisfaction and a sense of accomplishment, rather than external rewards.

Find sources of inspiration, such as role models, books, or motivational talks, to keep your enthusiasm and commitment high. Treat yourself with the same kindness and compassion you would offer a friend. Acknowledge your efforts and remind yourself that growth takes time. Let go of self-blame and guilt associated with setbacks. Forgive yourself and focus on moving forward with renewed determination.

Creating a Supportive Environment

Establish routines that support your physical, emotional, and mental well-being. Consistent habits can provide stability and a foundation for growth. Continuously seek ways to improve your routines and habits. Small, incremental changes can lead to significant long-term

benefits. Engage in collaborative learning experiences with others. Sharing knowledge and insights can enhance your understanding and foster a sense of community. Build and maintain networks of support, such as peer groups or professional associations, that provide encouragement and resources for growth.

CONCLUSION

Maintaining Self-Acceptance

In conclusion, you need to always reflect on your journey and see how far you have come that will encourage you to keep pushing and live a positive life without fear or doubt. You need to move forward with confidence so it will rub off onto others.

A better version of you is what you will be looking at every time you look into that mirror and you will embrace and cherish the person you have grown out to be, the shell would have come off of you. Opportunities will always follow you and you will make the most of it.

Reflecting on Your Journey

Identify key milestones in your journey toward self-acceptance. These could be moments of self-discovery, times when you overcome significant challenges, or instances where you embrace your true self. Reflect on the lessons you've learned along the way. How have these lessons shaped your understanding of yourself and the world around you?

Take pride in the effort and dedication you've put into your journey. Acknowledge the hard work and persistence it takes to embark on the path of self-acceptance. Express gratitude for the support you've received from friends, family, mentors, and even yourself. Recognize the positive influences that have helped you along the way.

Moving Forward with Confidence

With the foundation of self-acceptance firmly in place, it's time to look forward with confidence. Embrace the future with the assurance that you are equipped to navigate whatever lies ahead. Set new goals for personal development that align with your values and aspirations. These goals will continue to foster your growth and reinforce your self-acceptance. Commit to lifelong learning and remain open to new experiences and opportunities for growth.

Continue to build and refine your coping skills to handle future challenges with grace and resilience. Keep nurturing your support networks. Surround yourself with positive influences that uplift and encourage you. Live authentically by aligning your actions with your true self. Make choices that reflect your values and passions. Use your journey to inspire and support others. Share your experiences and offer encouragement to those who are also seeking self-acceptance.

Final Words of Encouragement

As you continue on your path of self-acceptance, remember that this journey is unique to you. There will be ups and downs, but each step you take is a testament to your courage and resilience. Stay committed to your journey. Self-acceptance is an ongoing process that requires consistent effort and reflection. Be patient with yourself. Growth takes time, and setbacks are a natural part of the journey.

Treat yourself with kindness and compassion. Celebrate your progress and forgive yourself for any perceived shortcomings. Encourage yourself as you would a dear friend. Remind yourself of your strengths and the progress you've made. Embrace your unique journey and the individuality that makes you who you are. Your path to self-acceptance is a powerful story of courage and resilience. Continue to grow, learn, and evolve. Your journey doesn't end here, it's an ongoing adventure filled with endless possibilities.

Parting Shot

You are not lost, neither are you an outcast, a thing, or whatever curse names you might have heard thrown your way. Just like anybody you are a human being. Stop worrying about who said what and worry about what you are gonna say to yourself once you realize the time you wasted living according to people's standard of living while depriving yourself of living. Take it easy, it's not the end but only the beginning of a new chapter of your life, do not waste it again, embrace it and be thankful for it.

Thank you for embarking on this journey with "Same Love, Mismo Amor: A Journey to Self-Acceptance." May you continue to grow, thrive, and inspire others with your story.
Stay blessed, continue to live and love, and above all keep shining.

THE END!!!!!

www.ingramcontent.com/pod-product-compliance
Lightning Source LLC
Chambersburg PA
CBHW070800250726
48662CB00004B/1909